Exploring Together

HOUGHTON MIFFLIN HARCOURT
School Publishers

Contents

Go, Jones! 2

So Much Fun 12

My Mule, Duke 22

At the Beach 32

Who Will Teach Us? 42

The King's Song 52

Ray Trains Dex 62

Sweet Treats 72

Let's Eat 82

It Was Snow Fun 92

Boat Rides 102

Rex Knows .112

Bedtime for Ray 122

Pancake Ran 132

Rosebud 142

Word Lists **152**

TEKS **1.3A** decode words in isolation; **1.3C(ii)** decode using open syllables; **1.3C(iv)** decode using VCe pattern; **1.3D** decode words with common spelling patterns

Phonics

Words with Long o Follow the path. Read the words. Where does the path go?

Go, Jones!

by Trey Barney

illustrated by Linda Chesak-Liberace

Jones woke up. It was time to
go, go, go! Jones will get Mike.

Mike had a bone.

"This bone is just for Jones," said
Mike. "It is just for him."

Jones ran to get his bone. Jones ran around and around. Then Jones went to dig in the sand.

Jones dug a big hole. What will
go in this big hole? The bone that
Mike gave Jones will go in it.

But look! A big, big bone is in
the hole! It is such a big bone.

Can Jones dig it up? Can Jones
carry it?

Jones went home to get Mike
because the bone was so, so big.
Mike can help Jones dig it up.

Jones ran and got Mike. Mike
dug and dug. So did Jones. Jones
rode home with the big, big bone.

What can that big, big bone be?

TEKS 1.9A retell story events; **ELPS** 4G demonstrate comprehension through shared reading/retelling/responding/note-taking

Retelling

Events Think about these events from "Go, Jones!"

- Jones and Mike dug up the big bone.
- Jones found a big, big bone in the sand.
- Mike gave a bone to Jones.

Work with a partner to put the events in the correct order.

TEKS **1.3A** decode words in context and in isolation; **1.3C(ii)** decode using open syllables; **1.3C(iv)** decode using VCe pattern; **1.3D** decode words with common spelling patterns

Phonics

Words with Long <u>o</u> Read each sentence. Point to and reread the long <u>o</u> words. Then match each sentence to a picture.

1. Jo is jumping rope.

2. I like that rose so much!

3. It will go up the pole.

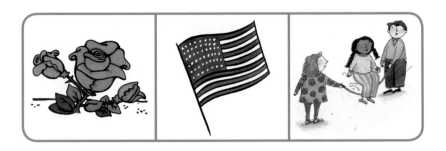

So Much Fun

by Rosarita Mencia
illustrated by Diana Schoenbrun

Before the sun rose, Jack got on
his bike. Jack rode and rode.

Jack rode his bike to Dan's home.
Jack had a note for Dan. Jack put
tape on his note and stuck it up.

14

Dan woke up. Dan put on his robe. Dan got Jack's note. Then Dan went back in with his note.

Meg woke up. Meg put on her
robe. Meg got Jack's note. Then
Meg went back in with her note.

16

Mo woke up. Mo put on his robe.
Mo got Jack's note. Then Mo went
back in with his note.

Mo,

Go to Big Pond.
Get to the pond
before 9:00.

Bring snacks.

Jack

Dan, Meg, and Mo sat. Jack got
up. Jack spoke.

"I will tell a joke," said Jack.

"Let's hope it is funny," said Mo.

Jack had so much fun telling jokes!
So did Dan. So did Meg. So did Mo.

TEKS 1.19B write short letters; **1.21B(iii)** capitalize names of people; **ELPS 5G** narrate/describe/explain in writing

Writing

Letters Think of something you want to tell a friend. Instead of speaking to your friend, write a note. Use Jack's note from "So Much Fun" as a model.

Remember Capitalize your name and your friend's name.

TEKS **1.3A** decode words in isolation; **1.3C(iv)** decode using VCe pattern; **1.3D** decode words with common spelling patterns

Phonics

Words with Short and Long

o and u Read each word pair. Tell each vowel sound you hear. Then use two of the words in a sentence.

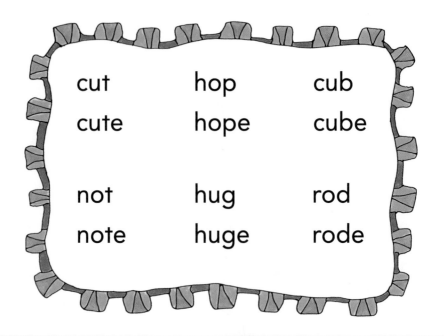

cut	hop	cub
cute	hope	cube
not	hug	rod
note	huge	rode

My Mule, Duke

by Richard Stemple

illustrated by
Jackie Snider

Duke is a big mule. Duke is a
huge mule. Duke lets June ride on
his back.

23

June is light. It is fun to sit on
Duke's back. Duke will carry June
home. They go clip, clop, clip, clop.

No! No! Duke sits down! June
must go home. Get up! Be a good
mule, Duke. Get up! Duke just sits.

What can June do? Duke just
sits. June must go home. Duke sits
still. Duke will not get up. June lets
Duke sit. June picks up the flute.

June can skip home. Skip, skip,
skip. June can hop home. Hop, hop,
hop. June can use the flute. June
makes a tune.

June will play a tune. June skips
to the tune. June hops to the tune.
Skip, hop, hop, skip, hop, hop.
June skips and hops to the tune.

Duke likes June's tune. Duke gets
up. Duke runs, clip, clop, clop, to
June. Duke runs, clip, clop, clop, to
the tune. Clip, clop, clip, clop.

June will play the flute. Duke likes June's tune. Duke will carry June home. Clip, clop, clop. Clip, clop, clop.

Fluency

Read Together

Sentence Types Read "My Mule, Duke" aloud with a partner. Then count the different types of sentences you see. Use the end marks as clues to tell you how to read each sentence. Read the story again.

Phonics

Words with Long <u>e</u> Read the words on the shells. Tell what letter or letters stand for the long <u>e</u> sound. Then read the words again and listen for the long <u>e</u> sound.

bean

we

seal

she

speech

tree

me

peach

jeans

32

At the Beach

by Elaine Sciofus

illustrated by David Sheldon

Pete is my best pal. We meet at the beach each week. We run and jump and yell. It's fun!

Pete is six. So am I. Pete has a green cap. My hat is green. We eat sweet peaches at the beach. Yum, yum, yum.

Then we take a walk. Pete and I
hunt for shells. We keep about five
shells each.

Then we sit by the sea. Pete gets his feet wet. My feet get wet, too. Splash, splash, splash! We don't go in the sea. It's fun to just get wet feet.

We dig holes. Dig, dig, dig! The
sea runs in them. The holes fill up
fast. We get wet sand.

We get a lot of wet sand. We
make a neat sand beast.

The sand beast is like an eel.
Maybe it's a snake! We run and
jump over it.

Then Pete has to go home. So
do I. We had lots of fun. We will
meet at the beach next week.

TEKS 1.28 share information/ideas by speaking clearly; **ELPS 3D** speak using content-area vocabulary

Speaking

Share Tell a partner what you would do if you could spend a day at the beach. Use these tips.

Speaking Tips

- Speak clearly and loudly enough to be heard.
- Do not speak too fast or too slowly.
- Use complete sentences.

TEKS 1.3A decode words in context and in isolation; **1.3C(ii)** decode using open syllables; **1.3D** decode words with common spelling patterns; **1.3E** decode words with inflectional endings

Phonics

Words with Long <u>e</u> Read each sentence and match it to a picture. Then point to and reread the long <u>e</u> words.

1. Dean helped me plant beets and beans.

2. We see three sheep sleeping.

3. Queen Jean eats cheese.

Who Will Teach Us?

by Forest Von Gront

Mom is teaching Beth about planting seeds. Beth makes holes. She plants seeds. Beth will water the seeds and see them grow.

Miss Kim is teaching Lin a tune.
Each week Lin meets with Miss Kim.
Lin can read each note. She can play
well.

Dad is teaching Sam how to swim. Dad is holding Sam while he kicks his feet. Sam will be so glad when he can swim.

Bob likes to teach kids how to
play this game. He meets with them
each week. He teaches them to use
their feet and kick.

Mom is teaching Reed and Pete
how to bake. She will teach them to
be safe. She is helping them place
drops on the sheet.

Nell's mom is teaching Nell how
to clean the car. Nell wipes it with a
mitt. Nell will clean it so it shines.

Gramps is teaching Bill about
fishing. Bill can hold his fishing pole
just like Gramps. Gramps tells Bill to
be still when fish are close.

Could you teach a friend? What could you teach?

TEKS 1.17A generate ideas for writing; **1.27B** follow/restate/give oral instructions; **ELPS 3E** share information in cooperative learning interactions

Directions

Read Together

Write Make a list of activities you know how to do. Circle one thing on your list you want to teach a partner.

Give Directions Tell your partner how to do the activity. Make sure your directions are clear. Then switch roles.

TEKS **1.3A** decode words in context and in isolation; **1.3C(i)** decode using closed syllables; **1.3D** decode words with common spelling patterns; **1.3E** decode words with inflectional endings

Phonics

Words with ng and nk Read the sentences. Match the pictures and sentences. Then point to and read the words with ng and nk.

1. The king will sit and think.

2. The queen sings sweet songs.

3. The prince reads long books.

The King's Song

by Clint Moscari

illustrated by Valerie Sokolova

"Singing is my best thing," said
King Ming. He sang to Queen Ling.
He sang sweet tunes.

At five, Queen Ling sat. King
Ming got set to sing his song, but no
tune came out. King Ming did not
sing his song.

"Don't be sad, King Ming," said Queen Ling. "Maybe a bird can help you sing." Queen Ling wrote this note: Needed: Bird that can teach King Ming to sing.

Red Bird came, but he had no
songs. Pink Bird came, but he had
no songs.

Then Green Bird came. He had
sweet, sweet songs. His songs made
King Ming and Queen Ling smile.
Then Queen Ling spoke.

"King Ming has lost his song. Can
you teach King Ming to sing?" asked
Queen Ling.

    "I think I can teach him as quick
as a wink," said Green Bird.

"I will bring him sweet notes
each time I come," said Green Bird.

In just a week, King Ming had his song back.

"Singing is my best thing," sang King Ming.

Fluency

Punctuation Marks Take turns reading "The King's Song" aloud with a partner. Use the end marks to help you read smoothly.

Pronoun I Find the letter **i** in the story. When is it a capital letter? Tell why.

Phonics

Words with Long <u>a</u> Read the words on the tray. Name the letters that stand for the long <u>a</u> sound. Use two of the words in a sentence.

wait   mail   stay

way   snail

clay   train   day

chain   play

Ray Trains Dex

by Angie Tubbman

illustrated by Shirley Beckes

"Sit," Ray tells Dex. Dex sits.
"Good dog!"

"Stay," Ray tells Dex.

At first Dex stays. He stays and waits when Ray tells him.

But then, Dex will not sit and
wait. He runs.

Dex runs fast. Ray and Dad run
as fast as Dex.

"Stop, Dex," yells Ray. "Sit! Sit!"
Dex sits and waits.

"I think I hear a dog whine," Dad
tells Ray. "Maybe it needs help."

"Go," Ray tells Dex. Dex runs. So
do Ray and Dad.

Dex sees a dog. The dog's tail is
going thump, thump. She is glad to
see Dex. Dex sniffs, sniffs, sniffs.

"This dog has a cut," Dad tells
Ray. "It is not a bad cut."

Ray sees a rock on the ground.

"I think she got cut on this rock.
Do you think so, Dad?" asks Ray.

Dad nods as he checks the cut.

69

Call Kay if you
find this dog.
555-1234

"She is not a stray dog," Dad tells
Ray. "She has a tag. We will get
her food. Then we will call and tell
Kay to get her dog."

Words

High-Frequency Words With a partner, write each of these words on two cards:

| first | food | ground | hear | find |

Word Game Place the cards face-down on a table. Take turns choosing two cards. Read the words. If they match, keep them. If they don't, put them back. Who can make the most matches?

TEKS **1.3A** decode words in context and in isolation; **1.3C(i)** decode using closed syllables; **1.3D** decode words with common spelling patterns

Phonics

Words with Long <u>a</u> Use these words to complete the rhymes: <u>mail</u>, <u>Kay</u>, <u>day</u>. Then point to and read all the long <u>a</u> words.

We went out to play.
We had fun all _____!

Here's a note from Gail.
It came in the _____.

This little cat was
a stray.
Now she's my
pet, _____.

Kay

Sweet Treats
by Cyrus Rutherman

Grapes are a sweet treat.
These kids like to snack on grapes
every day. Would you like a bunch
right now?

Grapes grow on big vines.
Grapes can be green. Grapes can
be red, deep blue, and black.

Lines and lines of grape plants grow in the ground. Grape plants need sun. Grape plants need rain.

Grapes stay on vines a long time. After a wait, grapes will be ripe. Grapes take time to get big and plump and sweet.

Ripe grapes cannot stay on vines. Ripe grapes need to be picked when it is time. Ripe grapes must be picked by hand.

Trucks bring grapes to shops and stands. Fresh grapes cannot stay on trucks. Grapes may rot if they stay too long.

See the sweet fresh grapes at this stand. Which fresh grapes would you snack on?

Kay has a huge tray filled with fresh green grapes. She can't wait, so she takes a big bunch!

"Yum! Yum! Yum!"

TEKS **1.4B** ask questions/seek clarification/locate details about texts; **ELPS** **4G** demonstrate comprehension through shared reading/retelling/responding/note-taking

Facts

Details   You can learn a lot of facts from the words and pictures in a story.

Make a list of facts you learned about grapes in "Sweet Treats." Then write some questions you have about grapes or other fruits.

TEKS 1.3A decode words in context and in isolation; **1.3C(i)** decode using closed syllables; **1.3D** decode words with common spelling patterns; **1.3G** identify/read contractions

Phonics

Contractions Read each sentence. Tell which picture it goes with. Then point to and read the contractions. Tell which words each stands for.

1. <u>I'll</u> get some hay.

2. <u>We'd</u> like to play!

3. <u>You'd</u> need this in the rain.

4. <u>She'll</u> paint a flower.

Let's Eat

by Robert Stewart
illustrated by John Segal

The day had ended. It was time to
eat. Nell had a plate filled with meat.

"It's time to get Ben," said Nell.
"He'd hate to be late."

While Nell was out, Fay came in.
Fay had a pot filled with rice. She
put rice on a plate.

"Nell likes rice and peas. She'll
like this," said Fay.

While Nell was out, Blaine came
in. Blaine had a pot filled with
beans. Blain put beans in a big dish.

"Ben likes beans. He'll like this,"
said Blaine.

Then Jess came in. Jess filled
each cup with grape drink.
"Nell likes grapes. She'll like this.
She will," said Jess

Nell and Ben came home.

"Isn't this a treat?" asked Ben.

"Yes, it is," said Nell. "I didn't
make this, but I know who did."

Nell gave Ben a note.

Please come quick.
Let's have fun.
Your pals,
Nell and Ben

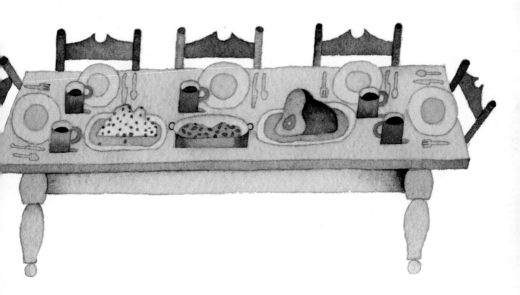

Nell set five gray plates and five
red cups. Ben went and got Fay,
Blaine, and Jess.

Nell, Ben, Fay, Blaine, and Jess had a fine meal.

"Let's clean up," said Jess.

Under each plate was a thank you note!

TEKS 1.3G identify/read contractions; **ELPS** 1H develop/expand learning strategies

Contractions

Remember Contractions are words that combine two words.

Reread Take turns reading "Let's Eat" with a partner. When you hear a contraction, raise your hand. Then have your partner tell which two words the contraction stands for.

TEKS **1.3A** decode words in context and in isolation; **1.3C(i)** decode using closed syllables; **1.3D** decode words with common spelling patterns

Phonics

Words with Long <u>o</u> Read each sentence. Reread the long <u>o</u> word and tell if it is spelled <u>oa</u> or <u>ow</u>. Match the sentence to a picture.

1. She's in the snow.

2. It's very slow.

3. It can croak.

4. It can make toast.

It Was Snow Fun

by Shira Alami

illustrated by Jamie Smith

Snow fell on the grass.   Snow fell
on oak trees.   Snow fell and fell.

Bill was sleeping when it snowed.
When he woke up the snow was
there. Bill got up fast. Bill likes
snow. He likes snow a lot.

Bill ran and woke up Joan. He
will show Joan the snow.

"Get up, Joan. Get up, get up!
It snowed, Joan!" said Bill.

Joan got up.

"We can get dressed and put on hats and coats. Then we can go and play in the snow," said Joan.

Bill fell in the snow on his back.
Joan fell in the snow, too. Bill made
snow wings. Bill and Joan had snow
all over them.

Bill made a little white snow cat.
Joan put a bow on it. It was cute.
"Can we make a snow dog,
Joan?" asked Bill when he was done.

98

"Not in this wind. It is blowing the snow. We must go in. Quick. Let's go!" said Joan.

"Yes," said Bill. "Let's go!"

"Did you have fun?" asked Mom.

"It was great when the wind didn't blow. Then it was snow fun!" said Bill.

Joan just laughed.

TEKS **1.1A** recognize that print represents speech; **RC-1(E)** retell/act out important story events
ELPS **1E** internalize new/basic academic language

Words in Print

Read Together

Dialogue Read the sentences.

> **Bill:** "It snowed, Joan!
> **Joan:** "Let's go play in the snow."
> **Bill:** "Get your hat! Get your coat!"
> **Joan:** "We can make a snow dog!"

Act It Out Now, with a partner, act out what Bill and Joan say.

101

Phonics

Words with Long o Read the words. Tell which words in each row have the long o sound. Then tell which two words rhyme. Which letters stand for the long o sound in each rhyming word?

1. low   coat   dot   crow

2. loaf   catch   show   know

3. flown   coach   groan   pitch

4. clock   throw   goat   grow

Boat Rides

by Redmond Turner

Is it time for a ride? A boat ride
can be so much fun.

This boat has sails as white as
snow. The big white sails make the
boat go. Wind blows and fills the
sails.

Strong winds can make the boat
go fast! It is fun to sail, but you
must stay safe. You need a life vest.

This flat boat has no sails. It
is slow. You use a pole to make it
float. It can carry loads down this
stream.

This boat is a raft. It is fun to
ride fast on white waves. Hats and
life vests help keep this ride safe.

This boat has no sail. It is not a
raft. To make this boat go you must
row. If you stop rowing, the boat will
just float and drift off.

This man rows with his left hand.
Then he rows with his right hand. He
will just keep rowing. Soon his boat
will pick up speed.

This boat is a huge ship. It can
take long trips at sea. If you were
on this ship, you could eat, sleep, and
play games on it. Would that be
great?

TEKS 1.14B identify important facts/details; 1.19C write brief comments on texts; **ELPS** 5G narrate/describe/explain in writing

Details

Important Details Think about the different boats you learned about in "Boat Rides." Choose one and draw a picture of it.

Write sentences to tell what you know about the boat. Would you like to have a boat like it? Write why or why not.

TEKS **1.3A** decode words in context and in isolation; **1.3D** decode words with common spelling patterns; **1.3E** read words with inflectional endings **1.3G** identify/read contractions

Phonics

Contractions Read each sentence and find the contraction. Match the sentence to a picture. Then read the sentences again. Tell which three words rhyme with <u>coat</u>.

1. We're looking at the goat.

2. I've started to float.

3. We're rowing the boat.

Rex Knows

by Paul Russell
illustrated by Susan Lexa

"Wake up," Joan tells Rex. "It's time for work."

Rex likes his job, so he gets up.

Joan fills each bowl.

"Eat up so you can do a great job," Joan hints as Rex eats.

"Stay still," laughs Joan. "Slow
down. We've no time to play. I must
brush your coat so it feels soft."

Then Joan gets her coat and the
leash. Rex and Joan go to work.
Joan knows that Rex likes his job so
much! Joan likes it, too.

On the way, Rex sees Nat and his dog Duke. Nat knows that Rex can't stop to play. Nat knows Rex must get to his job on time.

Joan stops and talks with Kate.

"So, is it time for work, Rex?"
asks Kate. "Must Rex go?"

"Yes, we're on our way," Joan
tells Kate. "We'll have fun."

Joan and Rex get to work. Rex
sits still while Joan rings the bell.

Ring, ring, ring. Soon Rick lets
Joan and Rex in.

Rex is good at playing. He can
do tricks and make each friend smile.
Rex knows they're glad to see him.

Decoding

Read Carefully Read these sentences.

> Spot eats a bowl of dog food.
> I brush her coat.
> I know she likes to play!

Think Did you read every word correctly? If a word is hard to read, use the sounds of the letters to figure it out. Also, remember if it looks like a word you have learned. Reread the sentences.

TEKS **1.3A** decode words in context and isolation; **1.3C(i)** decode using closed syllables; **1.3D** decode words with common spelling patterns; **1.3F** identify/read compound words

Phonics

Compound Words   Read the story.   Then reread each compound word.   Tell what two words form the compound word.

We ride to the lake with Granddad on Sunday. We stop and eat pancakes on the way. Then we go out in a sailboat. We see a rainbow!

Bedtime for Ray

by Tami Lo Verso

illustrated by Yvette Banek

It was bedtime. Ray didn't want
to go to bed yet. He wanted to play
his game. He wanted to win.

Ray is six. He can tell time. Ray's dad has a rule about bedtime. On a weekday, Ray's bedtime is at 8:00. It was that time.

So Ray went up the steps.
Shep went with him. Shep likes to
be with Ray, and Ray likes to be
with Shep.

Shep likes to watch Ray. Shep
gets in the bathtub to see Ray brush
his teeth. Ray can't let Shep do that.
Shep can't be in the tub!

Ray must try to get Shep out. So
Ray gets in the bathtub. Ray can't
lift Shep up, but he gets Shep out.
Shep grins as if it is a game.

At last, Ray gets in his bed. His mother reads him a nice bedtime tale. Shep is so big that he can't sleep on Ray's bed.

Shep can't get on Ray's bed, but
Shep has a rug. Shep sleeps on the
rug at Ray's bedside.

Ray's dream is about his game.
In his dream, Ray wins the game.
What do you think Shep's
dream is?

Words

High-Frequency Words With a partner, write each of these words on two cards:

mother try want watch what

Word Game Place the cards face-down on a table. Take turns choosing two cards. Read the words. If they match, keep them. If they don't, put them back. Who can make the most matches?

Phonics

Compound Words Read the words in each box. Copy the words in the red boxes. Add words from the blue boxes to make compound words. Read your list. What do the words mean?

rain	box
home	run
pan	bow
bath	cake
mail	robe

Pancake Ran

retold by George O'Neal
illustrated by Carol Koeller

At sunrise, Midge and Madge got
up. Midge and Madge made a big,
big pancake.

"This is just for me," said Midge.
"No, it is not," hissed Madge.
While Midge and Madge yelled,
Pancake jumped up.

Then Pancake ran out the door.
Midge and Madge ran after
Pancake. Midge and Madge did not
catch him.

Pancake ran down a hillside and
met Sheep.

"I will catch you," boasted Sheep.

"Midge and Madge did not catch
me," yelled Pancake as he ran. "You
cannot catch me, Sheep."

Pancake ran past an old windmill and met Goat.

"I will catch you," grunted Goat.

"Midge, Madge, and Sheep did not catch me," yelled Pancake. "You can try, but you cannot catch me."

Pancake sat on the roadside and rested.

"Where are you going?" asked Fox.

"I am going on a trip," said
Pancake.

"I cannot hear you," said Fox.
"Get close."

But, Pancake just ran.

Then Pancake jumped on a
sailboat with big white sails. He
sailed and sailed and sailed.

Compound Words

Remember A compound word is made up of two smaller words.

pan + cake = pancake

Reread Take turns reading "Pancake Ran" with a partner. When you hear a compound word, raise your hand. Use the small words to tell what the compound word means.

TEKS 1.3A decode words in isolation; **1.3D** decode words with common spelling patterns; **1.3F** identify/read compound words

Phonics

Words with Short e Spelled ea

Read each word to go up the steps. Find the compound words. Tell which base word has short e spelled ea.

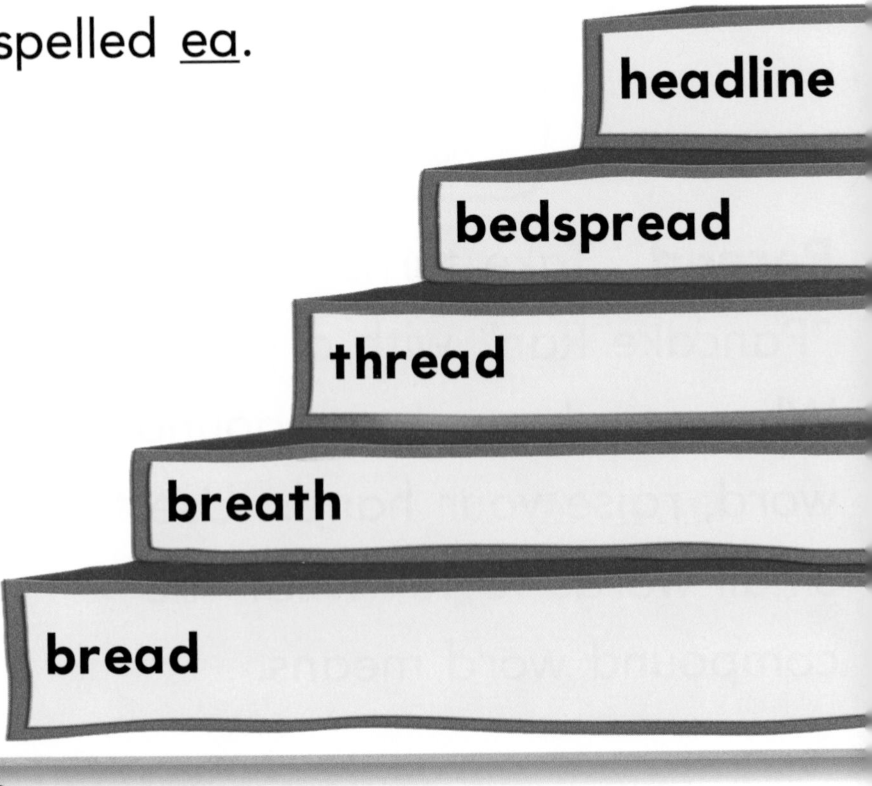

headline
bedspread
thread
breath
bread

Rosebud

by Mary Martinez
illustrated by Benrei Huang

My mother had a big white boat.
Mom's big white boat was an old
sailboat.   Mom let me name it.

I chose "Rosebud." Mom got red paint and paintbrushes. We painted that name on the boat. I painted a red rosebud.

Mom and I went sailing. We
sailed in the daytime. On nice days,
we set sail at sunrise. Sometimes we
sailed all day long.

If it rained, we stayed inside the
boat. We played games. We read.
But sailing was more fun than being
inside.

When the sun peeked out, we'd
go up and sit topside. The sailboat
rocked and we sang songs. We sang,
"Row, row, row your boat."

One time we went on a long trip.
We sailed and sailed. It was sunset,
but it was not bedtime yet.

The sun's rays spread. The sea glowed yellow and red. Then no more rays. The sun had set.

It was time to head to bed. It
was bedtime on Rosebud.

TEKS **1.18A** write brief stories; **1.21B(ii)** capitalize pronoun "I"; **1.21B(iii)** capitalize names of people

Writing

Plan and Write If you could go sailing, where would you go? Who would go with you?

Write a short story about a sailing trip you would like to take.

Remember Use capital letters for the word **I** and for names of people.

TEKS **1.3A** decode words in isolation; **1.3C(i)** decode using closed syllables; **1.3C(v)** decode using vowel digraph/diphthong patterns;

Phonics

Read to Review   Use what you know about sounds and letters to read the words.

Long e: ee

eel	see	tree	knee
week	green	three	queen

Long e: ea

eat	sea	leaf	east
dream	peach	beach	stream

Short Vowel Words with -dge

badge	fudge	budge	edge
judge	lodge	bridge	pledge

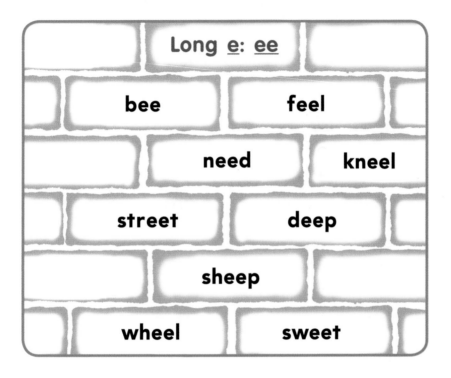

Long e: ee

bee   feel

need   kneel

street   deep

sheep

wheel   sweet

Short e: ea

head   deaf   read   bread

spread   thread   breath   health

TEKS **1.3A** decode words in isolation; **1.3C(i)** decode using closed syllables; **1.3C(v)** decode using vowel digraph/diphthong patterns; **1.3E** read words with inflectional endings;

Phonics

Read to Review Use what you know about sounds and letters to read the words.

Long a̱: a̱y

day	say	way	May
pay	play	gray	tray

Long a̱: a̱i

rain	pain	wait	tail
train	paint	chain	drain

Short e̱: e̱a

head	breath	bread	dread
thread	threat	sweat	wealth

Long <u>a</u>: <u>ay</u>

bay
days
hay
clay
tray
stay
sprays

Long <u>a</u>: <u>ai</u>

main
stain
paints
chains
waist
rain
sprain

Short <u>e</u>: <u>ea</u>

head
spreads
thread
health
wealth
bread
breath

TEKS **1.3A** decode words in isolation; **1.3B** apply letter-sound knowledge to create words; **1.3C(i)** decode using closed syllables;

Phonics

Read to Review Use what you know about sounds and letters to read the words.

Short e: ea

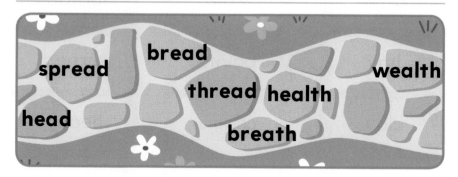

spread
bread
wealth
thread health
head
breath

Words with -dge

edge
bridge
lodge
badge smudge
judge
pledge

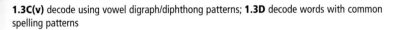

1.3C(v) decode using vowel digraph/diphthong patterns; **1.3D** decode words with common spelling patterns

Build and Read Words Put the letters together to read the words. Think of more words to add.

b ean	s ink
m ean	p ink
c l ean	th ink
m ow	b oat
r ow	c oat
g r ow	f l oat
d ay	r ain
s ay	m ain
p l ay	ch ain

157

Phonics

Decode Words in Isolation   Use what you know about sounds and letters to read each word by itself.

Long u: u-e

| tube | cute | huge | rude |
| use | mule | tune | cube |

Long o: o-e

| poke | tone | rope | mole |
| bone | home | pole | joke |

Long i: i-e

| Mike | pile | nine | write |
| knife | pine | bike | tile |

Phonics

Decode Words in Isolation   Use what you know about sounds and letters to read each word by itself.

Long u: u-e

use	rule	cube	dune
cute	tube	rude	huge

Long o: o-e

lone	pole	joke	rope
broke	hope	tone	hole

Long i: i-e

mile	pike	bite	like
nine	lime	write	mine

Phonics

Decode Words in Isolation Use what you know about sounds and letters to read each word by itself.

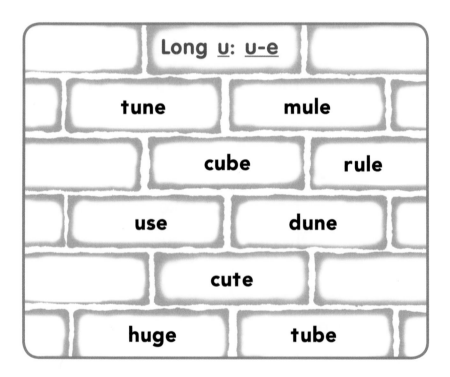

Long <u>u</u>: <u>u-e</u>

tune   mule

cube   rule

use   dune

cute

huge   tube

Phonics

Decode Words in Isolation Use what you know about sounds and letters to read each word by itself.

Long u: u-e

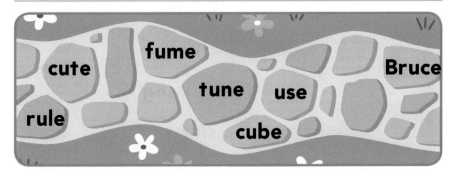

cute
fume
tune
use
Bruce
rule
cube

Words with kn, wr, gn, mb

know
write
numb
gnat
knot
wrist
thumb

Phonics

Decode Words in Isolation Use what you know about sounds and letters to read each word by itself.

Words with Final <u>ng</u>, <u>nk</u>

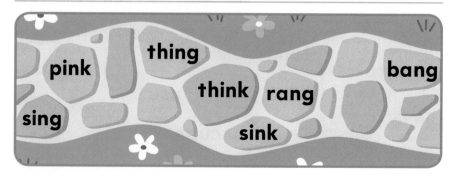

pink thing bang
think rang
sing sink

Long <u>u</u>: <u>u-e</u>

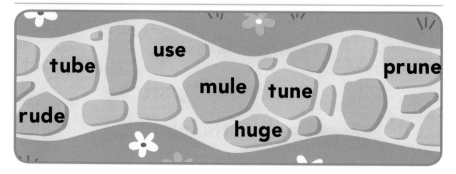

tube use prune
mule tune
rude huge

162

Word Lists

Accompanies
"Let's Go to the Moon"

Go, Jones!   page 2

Decodable Words
Target Skill: Long *o* (CV, CVC*e*)
go, Jones, woke, bone, hole, home, so, rode

Previously Taught Skills
and, big, but, can, did, dig, dug, gave, get, got, had, help, him, his, in, is, it, just, Mike, ran, sand, such, that, then, this, time, up, went, will, with

High-Frequency Words
New
around, because, carry

Previously Taught
a, be, for, look, said, the, to, was, what

So Much Fun   page 12

Decodable Words
Target Skill: Long *o* (CV, CVC*e*)
go, hope, home, joke, jokes, Mo, note, robe, rode, rose, so, spoke, woke

Previously Taught Skills
9:00, and, back, big, bike, Dan, Dan's, did, fun, get, got, had, his, in, is, it, Jack, Jack's, let's, Meg, much, on, pond, stuck, sun, tape, tell, telling, then, sat, snacks, up, went, will, with

High-Frequency Words
New
before, bring

Previously Taught
a, for, funny, her, I, put, said, the, to

My Mule, Duke

page 22

Decodable Words
Target Skill: Long *u* (CVC*e*)
Duke, Duke's, flute, huge, June, June's, mule, tune, use

Target Skill: Long *o* (CV, CVC*e*)
go, home, no

Previously Taught Skills
back, big, can, clip, clop, fun, get, gets, his, hop, hops, is, it, just, lets, likes, makes, must, not, on, picks, ride, runs, sit, sits, skip, skips, still, will, up

High-Frequency Words
New
carry, light

Previously Taught
a, be, do, down, good, my, play, the, they, to, what

At the Beach
page 32

Decodable Words
Target Skill: Long *e* (CV, CVC*e*) Vowel Pairs *ee, ea*
beach, beast, each, eat, eel, feet, green, keep, meet, neat, peaches, Pete, sea, sweet, we, week

Previously Taught Skills
an, and, am, at, best, cap, dig, fast, fill, five, fun, get, gets, go, had, has, hat, his, holes, home, hunt, in, is, it's, jump, just, like, lot, lots, make, next, pal, run, runs, sand, shells, sit, six, so, snake, splash, take, them, then, up, will, wet, yum

High-Frequency Words
New
about, by, don't, maybe

Previously Taught
a, do, for, I, my, of, over, the, to, too, walk

Who Will Teach Us?
page 42

Decodable Words
Target Skill: Long *e* (CV, CVC*e*) Vowel Pairs *ee, ea*
be, clean, each, feet, he, meets, Pete, read, Reed, see, seeds, she, sheet, teach, teaches, teaching, week

Previously Taught Skills
and, bake, Beth, Bill, Bob, can, close, Dad, drops, fish, fishing, game, glad, Gramps, he, helping, his, holes, is, it, just, kick, kicks, kids, Kim, like, likes, Lin, makes, Miss, mitt, Mom, mom, Nell, Nell's, note, on, place, plants, planting, pole, safe, Sam, shines, so, still, swim, tells, them, this, tune, us, use, well, when, while, when, will, wipes, with

High-Frequency Words
New
about, car, could

Previously Taught
a, are, friend, grow, hold, holding, how, play, the, their, to, water, who, what, you

The King's Song
page 52

Decodable Words
Target Skill: Final *ng, nk*
bring, King, King's, Ling, Ming, Pink, sang, sing, singing, song, songs, thing, think, wink

Target Skill: Long *e* (CV, CVC*e*) Vowel Pairs *ee, ea*
be, each, Green, he, needed, Queen, sweet, teach, week

Previously Taught Skills
and, as, asked, at, back, best, but, can, came, did, five, got, had, has, him, his, help, in, is, just, lost, made, no, not, note, notes, quick, Red, sad, sat, set, smile, spoke, that, then, this, time, tunes, will, wrote

High-Frequency Words
New
don't, maybe

Previously Taught
a, bird, come I, my, out, said, the, to, you

Ray Trains Dex

page 62

Decodable Words

Target Skill: Vowel Pairs *ai, ay*
Kay, Ray, stay, stays, tail, trains, wait, waits

Previously Taught Skills

555-1234, and, as, at, bad, but, checks, cut, Dad, Dex, dog, dog's, fast, get, glad, go, going, got, has, he, help, him, if, is, it, needs, nods, not, on, rock, run, runs, see, sees, she, sit, sits, sniffs, so, stop, tag, tell, tells, then, think, this, thump, wait, waits, we, when, whine, will, yells

High-Frequency Words

New
first, food, ground

Previously Taught

a, call, do, find, good, hear, her, I, the, too, you

Sweet Treats

page 72

Decodable Words

Target Skill: Vowel Pairs *ai, ay*
day, Kay, may, rain, stay, tray, wait

Previously Taught Skills

and, at, be, big, black, bring, bunch, can, cannot, deep, filled, fresh, get, grape, grapes, green, hand, has, huge, if, in, is, it, kids, like, lines, must, need, on, picked, plants, plump, red, ripe, rot, see, she, shops, snack, so, stands, sun, sweet, take, takes, these, time, treat, treats, trucks, vines, when, which, will, with, yum

High-Frequency Words

New
ground, right, these

Previously Taught

a, after, are, blue, by, every, grow, long, now, of, the, they, to, too, you, would

167

Let's Eat

page 82

Decodable Words

Target Skill: Contractions *'ll, 'd*
he'd, he'll, she'll

Target Skill: Vowel Pairs *ai, ay*
Blaine, day, Fay, gray

Previously Taught Skills
and, asked, be, beans, Ben, big, but,
came, clean, cup, cups, did, didn't, dish,
drink, each, eat, ended, filled, fine, five,
fun, gave, get, got, grape, grapes, had,
hate, home, in, is, isn't, it, it's, Jess, late,
let's, like, likes, make, meal, meat, Nell,
note, on, pals, peas, plate, plates, please,
pot, quick, red, rice, set, she, thank,
then, this, time, treat, up, went, while,
will, with, yes

High-Frequency Words

New
under, your

Previously Taught
a, come, have, I, know, out,
put, said, the, to, was, who,
you

It Was Snow Fun

page 92

Decodable Words
Target Skill: Vowel Pairs *oa, ow*
blow, blowing, bow, coats, Joan, oak, show, snow, snowed

Previously Taught Skills
and, asked, back, Bill, can, cat, cute, did, didn't, dog, dressed, fast, fell, fun, get, go, got, grass, had, hats, he, his, in, it, let's, likes, lot, make, made, Mom, must, not, on, play, quick, ran, sleeping, them, then, this, trees, up, when, white, will, wind, wings, woke we, yes

High-Frequency Words
New
done, great, laugh

Previously Taught
a, all, have, little, over, put, said, the, there, too, was, you

Boat Rides

page 102

Decodable Words
Target Skill: Vowel Pairs *oa, ow*
boat, blows, float, loads, row, rowing, rows, slow, snow

Previously Taught Skills
and, as, at, be, big, but, can, drift, eat, fast, fills, flat, fun, games, go, hand, has, his, hats, help, huge, if, is, it, just, keep, left, life, make, man, much, must, need, no, not, off, on, pick, play, pole, raft, rides, safe, sail, sails, sea, ship, sleep, slow, so, speed, stay, stop, strong, stream, take, that, time, then, this, trips, up, use, vest, waves, white, will, wind, winds, with

High-Frequency Words
New
great, soon, were, work

Previously Taught
a, carry, could, down, for, long, right, soon, she, to, would, you

169

Rex Knows

Decodable Words
Target Skill: Contractions *'ve, 're*
we're, we've

Target Skill: Vowel Pairs *oa, ow*
bowl, coat, Joan, knows, slow

Previously Taught Skills
and, as, asks, at, bell, brush, can, can't,
dog, Duke, each, eat, eats, feels, fills,
fun, get, gets, glad, go, he, him, hints,
his, in, is, it, it's, job, Kate, leash, lets,
likes, make, much, must, Nat, no, not,
on, play, playing, Rex, Rick, ring, rings,
see, sees, sits, smile, so, soft, stay, still,
stop, stops, tells, that, then, time, tricks,
up, wake, way, we, we'll, while, with,
yes

High-Frequency Words
New
great, laughs, soon, talk,
they're, work

Previously Taught
a, do, down, for, friend,
good, have, her, I, our, the,
to, too, you, your

Bedtime for Ray

page 122

Decodable Words
Target Skill: Compound Words
bathtub, bedside, bedtime, weekday

Previously Taught Skills
8:00, and, as, at, be, bed, big, brush, but, can, can't, dad, didn't, dream, game, get, gets, go, grins, has, he, him, his, if, in, is, it, last, let, lift, likes, must, nice, on, play, Ray, Ray's, reads, rug, rule, see, Shep, Shep's, six, sleep, sleeps, so, steps, tale, teeth, tell, that, think, time, tub, up, went, with, win, wins, yet

High-Frequency Words
New
mother, try, want, wanted

Previously Taught
a, about, do, for, out, the, to, was, watch, what, you

Pancake Ran

page 132

Decodable Words
Target Skill: Compound Words
cannot, hillside, pancake, roadside, sailboat, sunrise, windmill

Previously Taught Skills
am, an, and, as, asked, at, big, boasted, but, catch, close, did, Fox, get, Goat, going, got, grunted, he, him, hissed, is, it, jumped, just, made, Madge, me, met, Midge, up, this, no, not, on, past, ran, rested, sailed, sails, sat, Sheep, then, trip, up, while, white, will, with, yelled

High-Frequency Words
New
door, old, try

Previously Taught
a, after, are, down, for, hear, I, out, said, the, where, you

171

Rosebud

Decodable Words

Target Skill: Short Vowel /e/ea
head, read, spread

Target Skill: Compound Words
bedtime, daytime, inside, paintbrushes, Rosebud, rosebud, sailboat, sunrise, sunset, topside

Previously Taught Skills
an, and, at, bed, being, big, boat, but, chose, day, days, fun, games, glowed, go, got, had, if, in, it, let, long, me, Mom's, Mom, name, nice, no, not, paint, painted, on, peeked, rained, rays, red, rocked, row, sail, sailed, sailing, sang, sea, set, sit, songs, stayed, sun, sun's, than, that, then, time, trip, up, we, we'd, went, when, white, yet

High-Frequency Words

New
more, mother, old

Previously Taught
a, all, I, my, one, out, sometimes, the, to, was, yellow, your